ANCIENT GREEKS

Anita Ganeri

STARGAZER BOOKS
Mankato, Minnesota

How to use this book

The key below shows the separate subject areas in this book. Included are Ancient Greek history, as well as literature, science and math projects, geographic facts, and the Arts.

Introduction

Among the city-states of Ancient Greece, the seeds of Western civilization were sown. The Greeks' pioneering work in science, philosophy, and the arts continues to influence our lives today. *Demokratia*, the concept of allowing ordinary men a say in the running of their town, is a Greek invention. It still forms the basis of many governments today.

Created and produced by
Aladdin Books Ltd

First published in 2010
in the United States by
Stargazer Books,
distributed by
Black Rabbit Books
P.O. Box 3263
Mankato, MN 56002

Design   Omnipress Ltd
Designer   Vivian Foster
Illustrators Peter Kesteven,
              Dave Burroughs,
              Sergio Momo

Printed in the United States

The author, Anita Ganeri, M.A., has written many books for children on history, natural history, and other topics.

The historical consultant, Dr. Anne Millard, has written many books for children on history and archaeology.

   Library of Congress Cataloging-in-Publication Data
Ganeri, Anita, 1961-
  The Greeks / Anita Ganeri.
     p. cm. -- (All about ancient peoples)
  Includes index.
  ISBN 978-1-59604-204-9
  1. Greece--Civilization--To 146 B.C.--Juvenile literature. I.
Title.
  DF77.G2192 2009
  938--dc22
                2008016506

Geography

The symbol of planet Earth indicates where geographical facts and activities are included. These sections look at how the Ancient Greeks influenced other parts of the world.

Language and literature

An open book symbolizes activities that involve language. These sections explore some of the many myths and legends in Ancient Greece, including the fearsome Minotaur.

Science and math

The microscope symbol shows where science, math, or natural history information is given. Many of the names used today for plants or animals are Greek in origin. Also discussed are the Ancient Greeks' advances in medicine.

History

The scroll and the hourglass indicate where historical information is given. These sections look at events in Ancient Greek history, and examine the impact of Greek culture on our society today.

Social history

The symbol of the family shows where information about social history is given. These sections look at the everyday lives of the Ancient Greeks, their food, and the clothes they wore.

Arts, crafts, and music

This symbol gives details about the arts, crafts, or musical activities of the Greeks. Greek architecture has been copied throughout the world. Some of its styles are shown here. Their love of music is also discussed.

Contents

The Island Kingdom

Greece consists of a mountainous area of mainland and hundreds of islands in the Ionian and Aegean Seas. In ancient times it also included colonies in Asia Minor (modern-day Turkey). The first major civilization in this area had developed on the largest island, Crete, by about 2000 BC. It is called the Minoan civilization, after its ruler, King Minos. The Minoans flourished from 2000–1450 BC and became a very wealthy kingdom.

Date Chart

c.3000–1000 BC The Bronze Age in Crete and Greece. People discover how mix tin and copper to make bronze for weapons and tools.
c.2600–2000 BC The people of the Cyclades Islands become prosperous.
c.2000–1450 BC The Minoan civilization on Crete is at the height of its powers.
c.1900 BC The first Minoan palaces are built.
c.1700 BC The palaces are destroyed by earthquakes and later rebuilt.
c.1450 BC Crete is invaded by the Mycenaeans.
c.1100 BC The Mycenaean way of life breaks down.
AD 1894 Sir Arthur Evans discovers the ruins of Knossos.

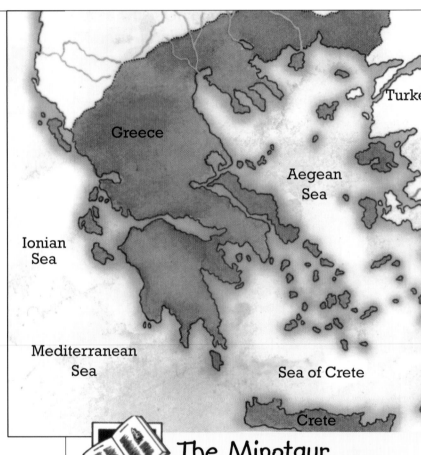

The map above shows the extent of Greek territory (in brown) during the Minoan Period.

The main stairway of the Minoan Palace at Knossos

The Minotaur

According to legend, the Minotaur was a horrible monster, half man, half bull, who lived in the labyrinth of Crete. Young girls were thrown into the labyrinth for him to eat. There was no escape as the labyrinth was like a maze.

Knossos

Many Minoan towns were built around splendid palaces, such as the one found at Knossos (below). This palace would have housed thousands of people. It was well organized, with an efficient water supply and drainage system. There were royal apartments, workshops, and storehouses.

Knossos was also used as a trading center. Trade was based on wine, grain, and olive oil.

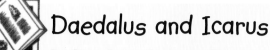

Daedalus and Icarus

In Greek mythology the inventor Daedalus and his son, Icarus, were exiled from the mainland. They fled to Crete where King Minos ordered them to build the labyrinth to house the Minotaur.

When Daedalus helped Minos' daughter, Ariadne, to escape with Theseus, the slayer of the Minotaur, Minos imprisoned both father and son. In an attempt to escape, Daedalus made each of them a pair of wings out of feathers and wax. The wings were a success and Daedalus flew to freedom. Icarus, however, flew too close to the sun. The wax melted and he plunged into the sea and drowned.

Palace frescoes

The walls of Knossos were covered in frescoes (paintings done on wet plaster). Only fragments of the originals survive, but they give valuable information about Minoan lifestyle. The dolphin, below, comes from the Queen's apartment.

The bull and the ax

The two main sacred symbols used by the Minoans were a pair of bull's horns and a double-headed ax (below), called a *labrys*. King Minos was thought to have been the son of the god Zeus and a princess called Europa. To bring her back to Crete, Zeus turned into a bull and carried her on his back.

5

Mycenaean to Archaic

The Mycenaeans dominated mainland Greece from 1600–1200 BC. They lived in small, separate kingdoms, but shared the same language and way of life. They were great warriors and traders, but their world entered a period of decline in 1200 BC, called the Dark Ages. This was followed by the Archaic Period, which brought renewed prosperity to Greece.

Date Chart

c.1600–1200 BC The Mycenaeans dominate mainland Greece.
c.1250 BC Traditional date for the Trojan War.
c.1100–800 BC The Dark Ages in Greece. The art of writing, known to both the Minoans and the Mycenaeans, is lost.
c.1100 BC The Dorian Greeks come to prominence.
c.800–500 BC The Archaic Period. A new system of writing is adopted.
c.750–650 BC Overcrowding and lack of farmland at home leads many people to leave Greece and establish Greek colonies around the Mediterranean and in Asia Minor.
776 BC The first Olympic Games are held at Olympia.

■ Greek homeland
■ Colonies settled

Soldiers on the ramparts defended the palace from attack.

Tomb interior (above)

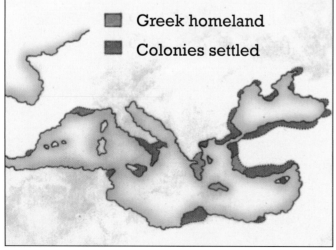

By about 1500 BC, huge, beehive-shaped tombs were being built for the kings of Mycenae. The stones were laid in circles and cut to form a dome. The whole tomb was then covered in earth. Early historians thought that the tombs must be treasuries as they contained so many grave goods.

Grave circle

Excavations in the 19th century of Mycenae ruins revealed a graveyard where members of the Mycenaean royal family were buried. The graves were full of possessions (top left) and surrounded by a low, circular wall.

The Lion Gate was the main entrance to Mycenae. Two huge lions were carved above the gateway.

Like the Minoans, the Mycenaeans based their cities, and their economy, around palaces. The heavily fortified palace complex was built on top of a hill so that it could be easily defended from attack. This type of city was known as an *acropolis* or "high city." It was surrounded by stone walls 15 ft (5 meters) thick.

The Argonauts

The spirit of travel and adventure in Ancient Greece is reflected in the legend of Jason and the Argonauts. Jason's quest was to fetch the golden fleece from the city of Colchis in order to reassert his claim to the throne of Iolchus. He set off in his ship, the *Argo*, with a band of heroes, the Argonauts. Despite facing many hazards, Jason succeeded in his crusade.

Achilles' heel

A person's weak spot is sometimes referred to as their Achilles' heel. In legend, the hero Achilles was dipped into the river of immortality as a baby. He died, however, from a wound to his heel, where his mother had held him.

The Trojan War

According to the poet Homer, a Trojan prince called Paris fell in love with Helen, the beautiful wife of the King of Sparta. Paris carried her off to Troy. The Mycenaeans swore revenge. After a 10-year-long siege, they tricked the Trojans into taking a large wooden horse into their city, unaware that it was full of Mycenaean soldiers.

Society and Law

By the 700s BC, Greece was divided into small, independent city states. Greek society was made up of citizens (men who were born in the city state) and noncitizens (women, foreigners, and slaves). Most city states were governed by an oligarchy—a small group of rich noblemen, called aristocrats. Resentment of their power, however, led to revolt. In 508 BC, a different system called democracy was introduced in Athens. It gave all male citizens a say in the government.

A woman's place

In Ancient Greece, women were thought of as noncitizens. They were controlled by men and could not take part in the running of the city. Greek women usually got married at about the age of 15. The marriage was arranged and the husband was usually much older than his bride. A woman's role was to look after the house, spin and weave cloth, and raise the children.

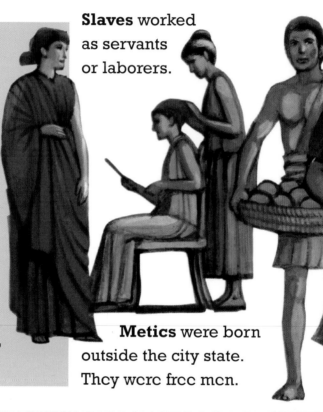

Slaves worked as servants or laborers.

Metics were born outside the city state. They were free men.

Aristotle

Greek *gymnasia*

In Greece, a *gymnasium* was a center for sport and learning. Apart from training facilities, there might also have been a library and a lecture hall. In the 4th century BC, the philosopher Plato and his brilliant pupil, Aristotle, taught in the colonnades of *gymnasia* throughout Athens. They both eventually founded their own schools, which became very famous. Plato's school was called the Academy; Aristotle's was called the Lyceum.

Citizens

were the most privileged social class in Ancient Greece. Only citizens could take part in the government of their city state, own land, or speak in a law court.

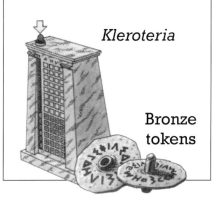
Education

In Athens, there were three types of schooling. A teacher called a *grammatistes* taught reading, writing, and arithmetic; a *kitharistes* taught music and poetry; a *paidotribes* taught athletics. It was only the sons of wealthier citizens who could afford a higher education. Girls were taught domestic duties at home by their mothers.

Changing fashions

The basic dress for men and women in Ancient Greece was a *chiton* (tunic), *himation* (cloak), and leather sandals. There were two basic styles of women's dress. The Doric chiton was wrapped around the body, while the Ionic chiton (below) fastened at the shoulders. Hair styles changed over the years, but curly hair was the fashion during the Hellenistic Period.

Athens and Sparta

Athens and Sparta were the two most powerful city states in Ancient Greece. From about 479–431 BC, Athens enjoyed a period of great prosperity known as the Golden Age. Science, philosophy, and the arts flourished, as did democracy under the statesman Pericles. Sparta was an oligarchy, led by two kings. There was intense rivalry between Athens and Sparta.

The city of Athens is dominated by the Acropolis hill, with the Parthenon temple complex on the top. In 480 BC, Athens was destroyed by the Persian army. After the Persians were defeated, Pericles ordered that the city be rebuilt. The Parthenon was constructed between 447–438 BC.

Kitchen

Altar

Andron

Workshop

Pots of life

Much of what we know about the Greeks comes from their pottery. Pots were often decorated with scenes of everyday life. These tell us about Greek fashion, homes, work, and religion. There were many different sizes, shapes, and styles of pots, depending on their use. The *Amphorae*, for example, were used to store oil and wine.

Most Greek houses, like those in Athens, above, were fairly simple buildings made of sun-dried mud bricks. Wealthier Greeks built their houses around central courtyards, where a well would provide water. Men entertained their friends in the *andron*, at the front of the house.

Athens and Athene

According to legend, Athens was named after the goddess of war and wisdom, Athene (below). She beat the sea god, Poseidon, in a contest to see whose name the city would take. Each had to offer something to the city.

Athene's gift of an olive tree, providing fruit and oil, was considered more valuable than Poseidon's promise of rich sea trade, and so she won. The contest is said to have taken place on top of the Acropolis. The temple complex was later built on this special spot and is dedicated to Athene.

Like most big cities, Athens had a bustling market place, called the *agora*. People came here to buy and sell goods, and to meet up with their friends.

Training Spartan style

Life was very different in Sparta. Every Spartan male had to train to become a soldier. At the age of seven, boys were sent to military camp. Conditions were harsh and discipline was strict. The boys were kept hungry and had to steal food to make them more cunning. As a result, the Spartans had a reputation for being the toughest warriors in Greece.

Babies were checked at birth. Weak babies were left to die.

Boys joined the military at age 20.

All Spartan girls played sports.

11

Trade and Commerce

The warm, dry climate and mountainous countryside of Greece meant that there was a lack of good farmland for crops. Although about half the population worked on the land, Greece was not self-sufficient and relied on trade to survive. There was also a widespread slave trade.

All change

The first coins were made at the end of the 7th century BC in Lydia, Asia Minor. The use of coins soon spread to Greece, and each city state minted its own. These were stamped with the city's emblem, for example, an owl for Athens, or with a god or hero, and later with the head of a ruler.

Coin from Athens 300–290 BC

Gold coin from 360–350 BC

Coin from Hellenistic Egypt

The map below shows Greece's main trading partners and its major imports. Merchants traded among other countries, the Greek colonies, and the city states. The most essential import was grain, much of which came from Greek colonies around the Black Sea. Athens imported about two thirds of its grain from abroad. Major exports from Greece included wine, olive oil, and pots.

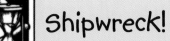

Shipwreck!

The wreck of a 4th century BC Greek merchant ship was found 90 feet (30 m) underwater near the ancient harbor of Kyrenia, Cyprus. It contained 400 *amphorae* from Rhodes and Samos, and a large cargo of almonds. Archaeologists found the remains of the crew's food—grape pips, garlic, fig seeds, and olive pits.

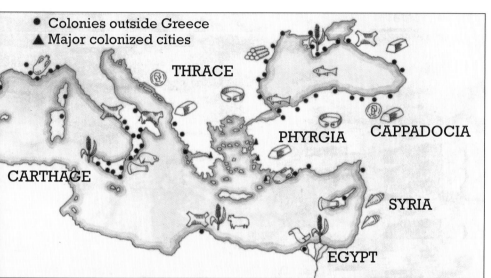

- Colonies outside Greece
- ▲ Major colonized cities

THRACE

PHYRGIA

CAPPADOCIA

CARTHAGE

SYRIA

EGYPT

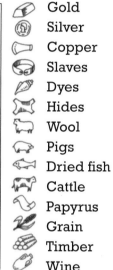

🖑	Gold
🖑	Silver
🖑	Copper
🖑	Slaves
🖑	Dyes
🖑	Hides
🖑	Wool
🖑	Pigs
🖑	Dried fish
🖑	Cattle
🖑	Papyrus
🖑	Grain
🖑	Timber
🖑	Wine

Weights and measures

In the *agora*, special officials called *metronomoi*, made sure that the traders used the correct weights and measures and gave people a fair deal. A trader's weights were tested against an official set of weights (like the ones below) to make sure that the trader wasn't cheating. Inspectors, called *agoranomoi*, also acted as quality controllers, checking the standard of the goods.

Greek food

The Ancient Greeks ate fairly simple food—bread and porridge, olives, olive oil, figs, poultry, and cheese. They made cheese from sheep's or goat's milk, which they also drank. Wine was their most popular drink. Breakfast might be bread dipped in wine.

The Wisdom of Greece

The Ancient Greeks were great scholars and teachers, and many of their ideas and theories still affect our lives today, over 2,000 years later. By the 6th century BC, people started to question the world around them. These scholars became known as philosophers, which in Greek means "lovers of knowledge." Great advances were also made in medicine, astronomy, history, geography, and math.

The most important philosophers were Socrates (*above*), Plato, and Aristotle. Socrates (c.469–399 BC) taught by questioning his pupils' arguments and exposing weaknesses in them. He was greatly respected by his pupils, who included Plato. However, the authorities were suspicious of his teachings and he was forced to commit suicide. Plato's greatest pupil was Aristotle (384–322 BC), whose works on science and biology were accepted as the authorities on these subjects for over 1,000 years.

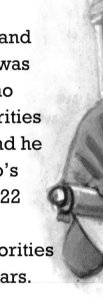

Hippocrates and medicine

Asclepius (*right*) was the Greek god of healing. Sick people prayed to him to cure them. A doctor called Hippocrates (c.460–377 BC) took a more practical and scientific approach to medicine. Patients were examined and a diagnosis was made. Then they were treated with herbal medicines, a special diet, and told to rest. Hippocrates wrote about how doctors should behave. Doctors today still follow a code of ethics called the Hippocratic Oath. The study of medicine flourished at the Museum (*Mouseion*) in Alexandria, Egypt, which became the center of Greek scholarship. The study of anatomy was pioneered by a scholar named Herophilus. Another scholar, Erasistratus, made similar advances by studying the circulation of blood.

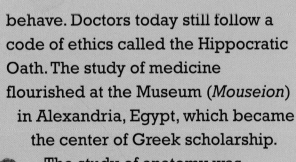

Eureka!

One of the most famous scholars at the Museum in Alexandria was the mathematician Archimedes. His theory of buoyancy, called the Archimedes Principle, came to him when he noticed how much water was displaced as he got in the bath. He is said to have jumped out of the bath shouting "Eureka! Eureka!" ("I've got it! I've got it!") Another of his inventions was an irrigation machine (*below*).

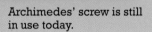

Archimedes' screw is still in use today.

Historians

The first Greek historians started writing after the Persian Wars in the 5th century BC. Herodotus (c.484–420 BC), often called "the father of history," wrote about the wars and his travels. Xenophon (c.430–354 BC) had been a commander in the Spartan army, and wrote about the Persian Wars and the history of Greece. Thucydides (c.460–396 BC) wrote a history of the Peloponnesian War. He used his own experience of fighting and information gained from interviews he conducted with other soldiers.

Plato's republic

Plato (c.428-347 BC) was a pupil of Socrates. When Socrates died, Plato wrote *The Apology* in defense of his teacher. He also wrote up many of Socrates' ideas in the form of dialogues between teacher and pupil. Plato is best remembered for his work called *The Republic*, which looked at the ideal forms of government and how they could be achieved. Plato's ideas are still influential today.

ΣΕΡΒΙΡΕΤΑΙ
ΠΡΩΙΝΟ ΚΟΜΠΛΕ

Language and Writing

The Ancient Greeks all spoke the same language, but different areas had different dialects. In Athens, people spoke a dialect called Attic. Attic was used mainly when writing Greek. The Greek alphabet *(below)* is based on that of the Phoenicians, who traded with the Greeks in the 8th century BC. The Roman alphabet, used in many western languages, is derived in turn from Greek.

Greek was first written from right to left like the Phoenician alphabet. Later on, the first line was written from left to right, the second from right to left, the third from left to right, and so on. Use Greek letters to write your own name.

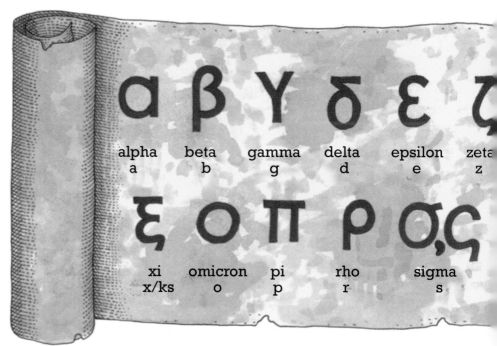

α β γ δ ε ζ
alpha beta gamma delta epsilon zeta
a   b   g   d   e   z

ξ ο π ρ σ,ς
xi   omicron   pi   rho   sigma
x/ks   o   p   r   s

Early writing

The Minoans of Crete had used a system of writing as early as about 2000 BC. This was a type of hieroglyphic (picture) writing. By about 1900 BC, they used a type of writing known as Linear A. Experts have been unable to decipher either type of writing, as so few examples of the script have survived for people to work on.

Linear A

Math sign

Greek letters are still used as mathematical symbols. The letter π (pi), for example, is used to work out the area or circumference of a circle. The theorems of many Greek mathematicians are still used in geometry, including Pythagoras' theorem on right-angled triangles.

Pythagoras' theorem states that the square of the length of the hypotenuse is equal to the sum of the squares of the other two sides.

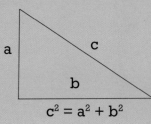

$c^2 = a^2 + b^2$

Epic poetry

Two of the most famous examples of Greek literature are the epic poems, *The Iliad* and *The Odyssey*. These long poems were composed by Homer sometime between 850–759 BC. *The Iliad* tells of the final stages of the Trojan War and of an argument between the hero Achilles and the leader of the Greeks, Agamemnon. *The Odyssey* tells of the many adventures faced by the Greek hero Odysseus.

A 2nd century AD copy of an original 2nd century BC bust of Homer

eta	theta	iota	kappa	lambda	mu	nu
e	th	i	k	l	m	n

tau	upsilon	phi	chi	psi	omega
t	u	t/ph	ch	ps	o

The Mycenaeans used Linear B (*right*) in about 1400 BC. Archaeologists have found tablets covered in this type of hieroglyphics among Mycenaean ruins. It was used mainly to keep records.

Natural names

Many of the words we use come from Ancient Greek. In nature, for example, the name 'hippopotamus' comes from two Greek words—*hippos* or "horse" and *potamos* or "river." So a hippopotamus is a "river horse." The rhododendron plant is a "tree of Rhodes"—*dendron* meaning tree.

Drama and Sports

The theater and sports played very important roles in the lives of the Ancient Greeks. Men took part in sports not only for fun, but to keep them fit for fighting. Athletic competitions, such as the Olympic Games *(see below),* were held on a local and national level. The theater in Greece grew out of the songs performed at a religious festival, the *City Dionysia,* in Athens. Soon huge, open-air theaters were built all over Greece.

The actors in a Greek play were men; women were not allowed to appear onstage. They wore masks to depict the characters they were playing. Theater-goers were given stone tokens that showed them where to sit.

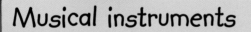

Musical instruments

Plays and poetry recitals were often accompanied by music. There were also songs for special events, such as births and deaths, marching songs for the army, and songs for religious festivals. Musical instruments included the *kithara,* a type of lyre which was played with a plectrum; a double set of pipes, called *auloi;* and the lyre. According to legend, the lyre was invented by the god Hermes, who made it out of the shell of a tortoise and the horns of an ox.

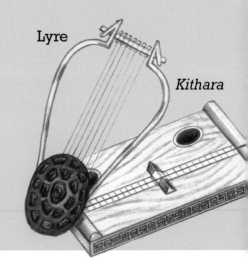

Lyre

Kithara

Olympic Games

Of the four national sports festivals held in Ancient Greece, the Olympic Games were the oldest and most important. They were held every four years in honor of the god Zeus. The first games took place in 776 BC. Athletes came from all over Greece to take part in events such as running, wrestling, the pentathlon, and throwing the discus. A truce was called between rival city states so that their athletes could attend. The winning athletes were treated like heroes.

A Greek bronze statue from the 6th century BC of a spartan runner

The Olympics today

The first modern Olympic Games were held in AD 1896 in Athens, 1,501 years after the last celebration of the ancient games. They were revived by a Frenchman, Baron Pierre de Coubertin, who was inspired by their ideals of sportsmanship. Many of the ancient traditions have been preserved. The modern games open with the lighting of the Olympic Flame. This is lit from a burning torch which has been carried by a team of runners from Olympia in Greece— the site of the ancient games. Athletes from more than 200 countries take part. The 2008 Games took place in Beijing. Vancouver is host in 2010.

Tragedy strikes

Greek tragedies written by playwrights, such as Sophocles, Euripides, and Aeschylus, are still performed in theaters all over the world. Almost all of the surviving tragedies are based on myths. According to Aristotle, tragedy had a special aim—to take away people's own feelings of fear or pity by involving them in the suffering of the play's characters. The play ends with the defeat of the main character by the hostile forces, and with his or her death. This was known as *catharsis,* "to cleanse."

Fun and games

Many types of toys and games were popular in Ancient Greece. Board games similar to checkers and chess were played. The Greeks also had a game similar to modern hockey. Knucklebones, which was popular with the women, was a game that was played with small animal bones. Children played with yo-yos, hoops, spinning tops, dolls, and balls.

Gods and Religion

The Ancient Greeks believed in many gods and goddesses who watched over them and controlled what happened in the world. The gods not only had many human characteristics, but they were also immortal. They were all-powerful and had to be honored and respected. The Greeks built beautiful, elaborate temples for their gods.

Festivals

Many festivals were held in honor of the gods. One of the biggest was the *Panathenaea* in Athens. It was held every four years and lasted for six days. On the final day, a huge procession carried a special dress up to the Acropolis for the statue of Athene.

Demeter, goddess of crops and the harvest, sitting on a panther

Bronze statue of Zeus (right)

The Greeks also worshipped the gods at shrines in their homes. Each day they said prayers at the family altar, which was usually in the courtyard of the house. As part of their worship, they poured an offering of wine over the altar (*shown right*). This offering was known as a *libation*.

Rich people were buried in a stone coffin, called a sarcophagus.

20

A Greek coin showing the head of Herakles

The gods of Olympus

Zeus Ruler of the gods and the heavens

Hera Sister and wife of Zeus; goddess of women and marriage

Poseidon Brother of Zeus; god of the sea

Pluto Ruler of the Underworld (Hades); god of the dead and brother of Zeus

Demeter Goddess of harvest and crops

Aphrodite Goddess of love

Ares God of war

Artemis Goddess of moon and hunting

Apollo Twin brother of Artemis; god of the sun, truth, and music

Athene Goddess of war and wisdom; patron goddess of Athens

Hermes Messenger of the gods; patron god of travelers

Hestia Goddess of the hearth; eventually left Olympus

Dionysus God of wine who took Hestia's place on Olympus

Oracles and cults

Before they did anything important, the Greeks liked to know if the gods approved. They might visit a soothsayer to find out what the future held, or ask a priest to read the omens. Sometimes they consulted an oracle, a shrine where the gods were supposed to speak through special priests or priestesses. The most famous was at Delphi. Here, the god Apollo spoke through a priestess, called the Pythia. There were also several mystery cults; the most popular one was the Demeter and Persephone cult.

Mount Olympus

At 8,750 ft (2,917 m) high, Mount Olympus, the home of the gods, is the highest mountain in Greece. It is visible from far down in the south of Greece, and from the sea. In ancient times, the gods were believed to live in great luxury on Olympus.

Death and the Underworld

The Greeks believed the souls of the dead went to the Underworld, or Hades. A coin was placed on a dead person's body to pay Charon, the ferryman, to take their soul to Hades. The person was then judged according to what sort of life they had led. Virtuous people went to the beautiful Elysian Fields, and bad people were sent to Tartarus. Those people whose lives fell somewhere in between went to the Asphodel Fields.

Elysian Fields

Tartarus

Asphodel Fields

Classical Greece

The Classical Period in Greece lasted from about 500–336 BC. Greek culture and military activity was at its height. In 490 BC, the Persians invaded Greece, starting a series of wars that lasted until 449 BC. Athens and Sparta joined forces to defeat the Persians. The Peloponnesian War began in 431 BC, and Sparta beat Athens. Sparta was later defeated by Thebes, in 371 BC.

Hoplites were foot soldiers in the Greek army.

The turning point in the Persian Wars was the Athenian victory in the great sea Battle of Salamis in 480 BC. The Greeks used warships called *triremes* (*above*).

Marathon task

The modern marathon race came about as a result of the Battle of Marathon in 490 BC. Marathon is situated about 25 miles (40 km) northeast of Athens. It was here that a Greek army defeated an invading Persian army. The Athenian general, Miltiades, sent a messenger back to Athens with news of their victory. The messenger, Pheidippides, ran the 25 mi (40 km) without stopping, and then dropped to the ground, dead.

Architectural style

Although Greek homes were quite simple in design, public buildings such as temples were often very grand. Columns were an important part of classical Greek architecture. Two main styles were used, the Doric and Ionic. Doric columns were sturdy and simple. Ionic columns were more elegant. In Roman times a third, more elaborate style, called Corinthian, also became very popular.

Doric

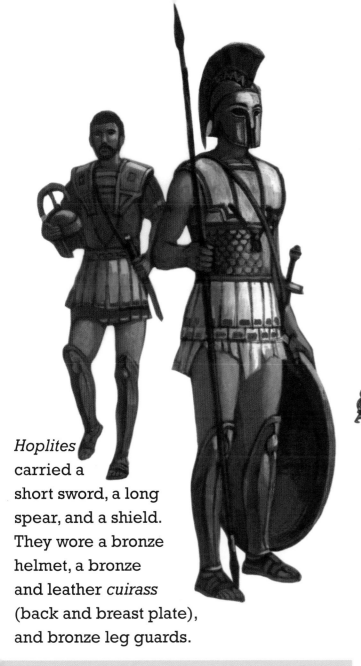

Hoplites carried a short sword, a long spear, and a shield. They wore a bronze helmet, a bronze and leather *cuirass* (back and breast plate), and bronze leg guards.

Ionic

Corinthian

Forming a phalanx

The most important battle formation was the phalanx. This was a rectangular block of *hoplites*, eight rows deep. In a battle, two opposing phalanxes charged each other until one gave way. It was important that all the soldiers marched in unison. If a soldier was killed or injured, the man behind stepped into his place.

Date Chart

500–336 BC Classical Period in Greece
490–449 BC The Persian Wars
490 BC Battle of Marathon
480 BC Battle of Salamis
478 BC Athens and its allies form the Delian League; Sparta and its allies form the Peloponnesian League.
479–431 BC Golden Age of Athens
431–404 BC Peloponnesian War
430 BC Outbreak of plague in Athens
371 BC Sparta defeated by Thebes at the Battle of Leuctra.
363 BC Athens and Sparta defeat the Thebans.

MACEDONIA

THESSALY

Aegean Sea

Persian Empire

Delphi

Thebes

Athens

Peloponnese

Sparta

CRETE

Athens

Sparta

Neutral states

Peloponnesian War

Alexander the Great

After the Peloponnesian War, the city states fought each other, while the king of Macedonia grew more powerful. In 353 BC, Philip II of Macedonia launched a successful campaign to gain control of Greece. He planned to lead a combined army of Greeks and Macedonians against the Persians, but he was assassinated in 336 BC. His son, Alexander, came to the throne.

The racing chariot on this gold coin refers to Philip II's success in the Olympic Games of 356 BC.

A gold coin from the reign of Alexander the Great which commemorates the victory at Salamis.

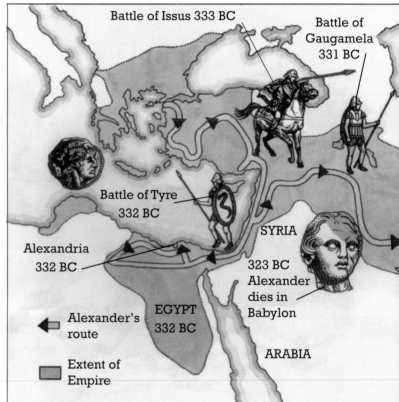

Battle of Issus 333 BC

Battle of Gaugamela 331 BC

Battle of Tyre 332 BC

SYRIA

Alexandria 332 BC

323 BC Alexander dies in Babylon

EGYPT 332 BC

ARABIA

Alexander's route

Extent of Empire

Philip II's reign began in 359 BC. He united the then struggling Macedonia, and transformed it into the greatest power of the day. Greek independence ended in 338 BC when they were defeated by Macedonia at the Battle of Chaeronea.

Alexander's empire was larger than any previous one, a third bigger than even the mighty Roman Empire. Alexander defeated the Persians in 333–331 BC. By 326 BC he had reached northwest India, but was forced to turn back by his battle-weary army.

Philip's tomb

In 1977, over 2,000 years after his death, Philip's tomb was discovered in the royal graveyard at Vergina, Macedonia. His cremated remains were found in a gold casket. Experts were sure it was Philip because he had a hole near the right eye socket, where he had been hit by an arrow.

Bust of Alexander the Great

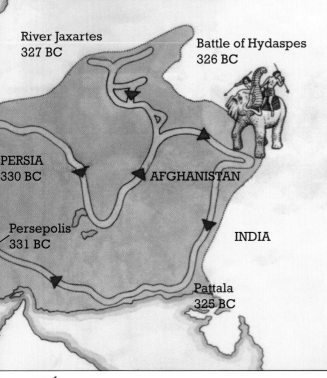

River Jaxartes
327 BC

Battle of Hydaspes
326 BC

PERSIA
330 BC

AFGHANISTAN

Persepolis
331 BC

INDIA

Pattala
325 BC

A town called Alex

Alexander founded many new cities and he called them all "Alexandria." The most famous Alexandria was in Egypt. Under Ptolemy, Alexander's successor, it became the country's capital. Its great marble lighthouse, the Pharos, was one of the seven wonders of the world.

Alexander wanted the people he conquered to feel part of the empire and not to resent their Greek rulers. To strengthen ties between the Greeks and the Persians, Alexander took to wearing Persian dress, and married a Persian princess called Roxane. He urged his soldiers to marry Persian wives.

Alexander was a great leader who was respected by his soldiers, because he marched as far and as hard as they did. When Alexander died in 323 BC, the empire was left in a state of chaos.

Greek influence on India

As Alexander's empire spread, so too did Greek culture, ideas, and style. They continued to influence the places conquered by Alexander long after his death. In India, Greek styles influenced art and sculpture, especially in the region known as Gandhara. Statues were carved with flowing robes, similar to those on Greek statues.

Persepolis palace

Persepolis was one of the greatest cities of the Persian Empire. It was founded in 518 BC by Darius I. During his reign, a splendid palace was built at Persepolis. Each year, festivities were held at the palace to celebrate the religious holiday of the New Year and to renew the king's divine rights. When Alexander captured the city in 331 BC, he burned the palace to the ground.

The End of an Era

When Alexander died, his baby son and half brother were appointed as his heirs. However, the real power lay in the hands of his generals, the *Diadochi*. Alexander's wife and heirs were murdered, and the empire was split among the *Diadochi*. Seleucus took control of Persia, Antigonas took Macedonia, and Ptolemy took Egypt. This period is known as the Hellenistic Period.

Date Chart

359 BC Philip II becomes King of Macedonia.
336 BC Philip is assassinated. His son, Alexander, becomes king.
333–331 BC Alexander invades and conquers the Persian Empire.
326 BC Alexander reaches India.
323 BC Alexander dies in Babylon.
The Hellenistic Period
323–281 BC The wars of the *Diadochi*; the empire is split into three kingdoms.
147–146 BC Greece and Macedonia become part of Roman Empire.
64 BC The Seleucid Empire in Persia is conquered by the Romans.
30 BC Egypt, the last Hellenistic kingdom, becomes a Roman province.

Map of Hellenistic world, 281 BC

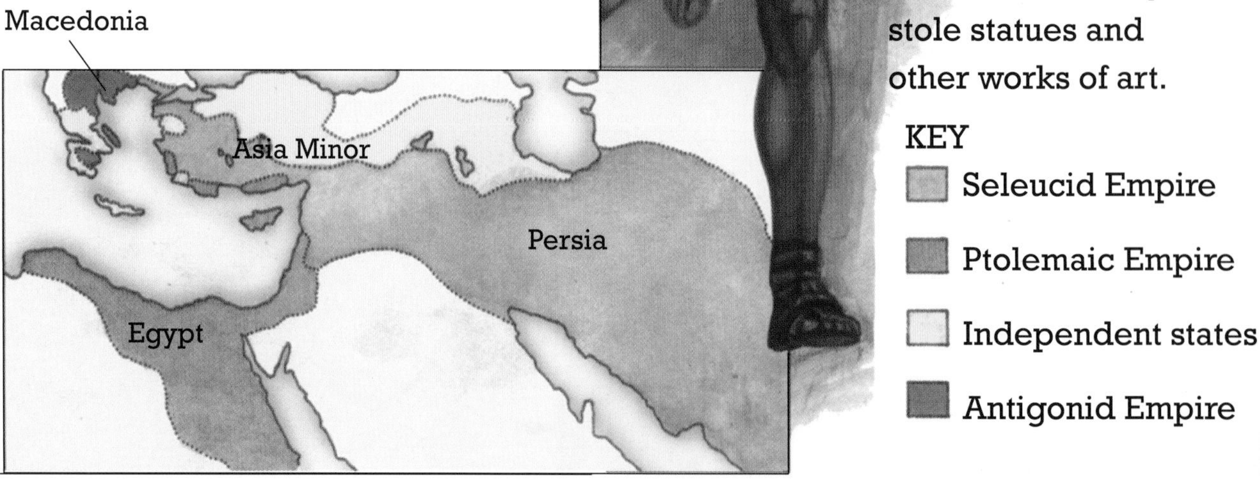

Macedonia

Asia Minor

Persia

Egypt

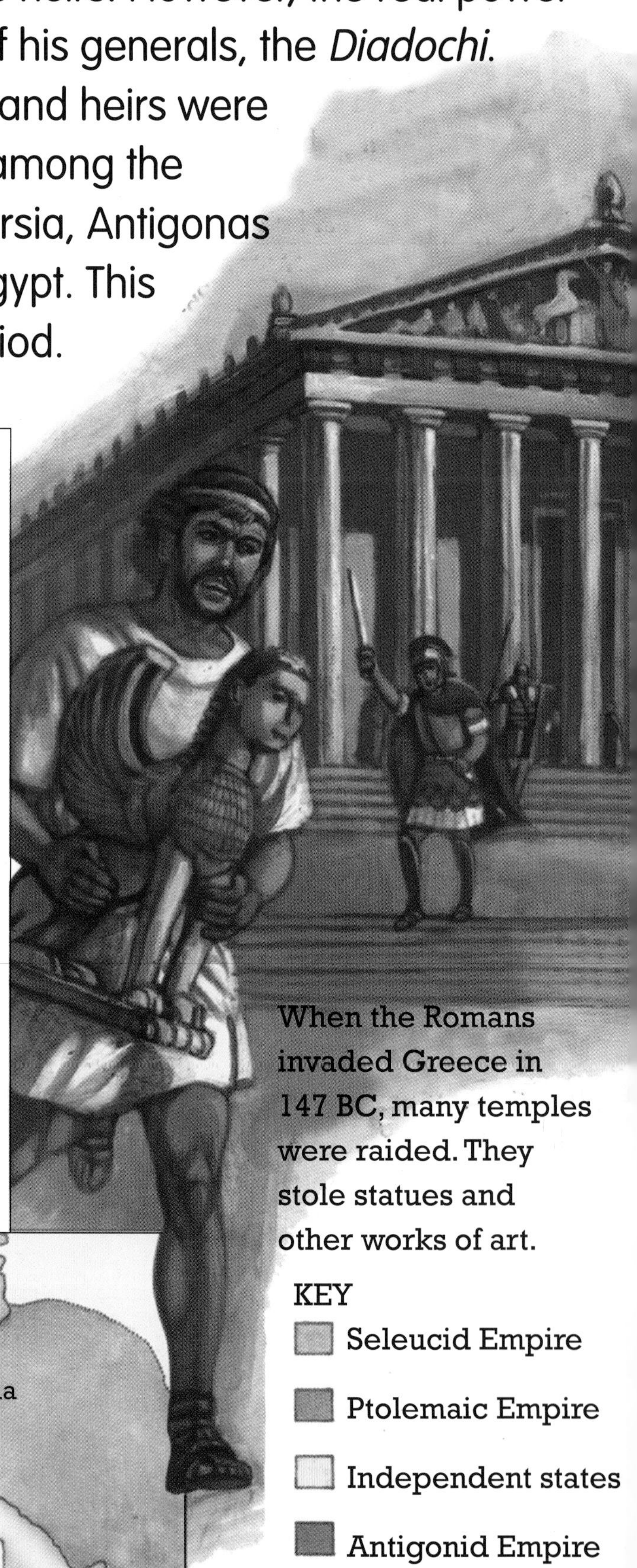

When the Romans invaded Greece in 147 BC, many temples were raided. They stole statues and other works of art.

KEY

Seleucid Empire

Ptolemaic Empire

Independent states

Antigonid Empire

Ptolemy was the most successful of Alexander's *Diadochi*. He and his successors, the Ptolemaic Dynasty, ruled Egypt from 323–30 BC. During this period, trade flourished in Egypt and the scholars of Alexandria kept Greek culture very much alive. Cleopatra VII was the last ruler of this dynasty. Despite her efforts to keep Egypt free from Roman rule, it became a Roman province in 30 BC.

The New Testament

During the Hellenistic Period, a form of Greek called *koine* was spoken all over the areas that Alexander had conquered. Jesus and his disciples spoke Aramaic, a non-Greek language, but their teachings were written down as the New Testament in *koine*.

Church of Santa Sophia, Istanbul

Roman art

Roman artists and architects borrowed many of their ideas from the Greeks. They also made copies of some of the best pieces of Greek sculpture. These have often survived where the originals have been lost.

Byzantium

In the 3rd century AD, the Roman Empire was divided into two halves—east and west. The Western Empire fell in AD 476, but the Eastern Empire survived until AD 1453. It was known as the Byzantine Empire. Its capital city was Constantinople (present-day Istanbul in Turkey). The Christianity practiced in Byzantium formed the basis for the Greek Orthodox Church.

The Legacy of Greece

The heyday of Ancient Greece was some 2,500 years ago. Yet the influence of Ancient Greek politics, philosophy, architecture, and language has remained strong in subsequent civilizations. Today we are always reminded of Greek influence through our democracy, language, science, medicine, and mathematics.

The Renaissance

During the Renaissance Period (15th–17th centuries), European writers, artists, sculptors, and architects turned to the craftsmen and scholars of Ancient Greece for inspiration. Examples include Michelangelo, Raphael, Leonardo da Vinci, and William Shakespeare. The French dramatist, Racine, was greatly influenced by the Greek writer, Euripides. Two of Racine's greatest plays are the tragedies *Andromaque* (Andromache) and *Phèdre* (Phaedra).

The theater today

Many of the Ancient Greek theaters remain remarkably well preserved. The theater shown below is at Dodona in northwest Greece. It was built between 297–272 BC, and could seat over 14,000 spectators. The horseshoe shape not only offered everyone an equal view of the stage, but also provided excellent acoustics. This forms the basis for our modern-day concert halls, theaters, and auditoriums. The auditorium at Dodona has been restored and is still in use.

The three basic styles, or orders, used by the Greeks (see pages 22/23) provide the inspiration for many modern buildings. The column from a building in London, England (below), can be seen to use the Ionic style of decoration.

Persephone and Hades banqueting in the Underworld (right)

The Parthenon in Athens (above left) is one of the best examples of Greek architecture. It was badly damaged in 1687 when Athens was taken over by the Venetians, who used the Parthenon to store gunpowder.

An explosion wrecked the central part of the building. The surviving sculptures were moved to the Acropolis Museum in Athens and the British Museum in London, where they can be seen today.

A mythical legacy

Many events were explained by the Ancient Greeks in terms of myths and the gods. For example, an explanation of the world's seasons can be found in the tale of Persephone, daughter of Demeter. Persephone was kidnapped by Hades, God of the Underworld. Desolate, Demeter searched the earth for her daughter, allowing the earth to become barren. Hades was eventually persuaded to return Persephone to Earth, but only for six months of the year.

Persephone's six months on Earth herald spring and summer, while her six months in the Underworld reflect Demeter's despair, and become winter and autumn. Today we have scientific theories to explain why certain things happen. Yet Greek myths remain a powerful source of inspiration for architecture, literature, painting, and music. Many of the stars, constellations, and galaxies also have names derived from Greek mythology.

c.3000–1000 BC
The Bronze Age

c.2100 The arrival of the first Greek-speaking people in Greece.

1900 First Cretan palaces built. Start of Minoan civilization on Crete.

c.1700 Cretan palaces destroyed by earthquakes; later rebuilt.

c.1600 Rise of Mycenaean culture.

c.1450 Cretan palaces destroyed. Mycenaeans take over the palace at Knossos and rebuild it.

c.1400 Knossos burns down.

c.1100–800 The Dark Ages.

c.800–500 The Archaic Period.

776 First Olympic Games held.

c.750–650 Greek colonies founded.

c.500–336 The Classical Period.

490 Persians invade mainland—defeated at Battle of Marathon.

480 Battles of Thermopylae and Salamis.

479 Battle of Plataea, Persians driven out of Greece.

431–404 The Peloponnesian War between Athens and Sparta.

359 Philip II becomes king of Macedonia.

336 Death of Philip, who is succeeded by his son Alexander.

323 Death of Alexander.

323–30 The Hellenistic Period.

323–322 Greek states lose their battle for independence.

8000 BC

First hieroglyphs (picture writing) in Egypt c.3500 BC

Old Kingdom in Egypt 2686–2150 BC

Pyramids built in Egypt during Old Kingdom

Egyptian Middle Kingdom 2040–1640 BC

2000 BC

Reign of Tutankhamun, the boy pharoah 1347–1339 BC

New Kingdom in Egypt 1552–1085 BC

Romulus and Remus found the city of Rome 753 BC

500 BC   Roman Empire c.27 BC–AD 476

Julius Caesar murdered 44 BC

Fall of the Roman Empire AD 476

Viking raids on Britain and France AD 793–1000

AD 1000   First Crusade to recapture Holy Land from Muslims AD 1096

First mechanical clock AD 1386

The Aztec Empire in Central America AD 1300s–1521

AD c.1200–1532 Inca Empire in South America

First cities—Jericho and Catal Hüyük 8000–5650 BC

Wheel invented by the Sumerians 3500–3000 BC

Rise of the Indus Valley civilization 2500–1700 BC

Early Minoan period in Crete begins c.2500 BC

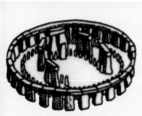

Stonehenge completed in England c.1500 BC

Destruction of Knossos in Crete. End of the Minoan period c.1400 BC

Shang Dynasty in China c.1766-1122 BC

Birth of Confucius 551 BC

Siddhartha Gautama, the Buddha c.500 BC

The Golden Age of Greece 479–431 BC

Alexander the Great conquers Persia, Syria, and Egypt 333–330 BC

The Qin Dynasty in China 221–206 BC

The Great Wall of China completed in 214 BC

Samurai warriors of Japan AD 1100s–1850

The Plague, or Black Death, spreads in Europe AD 1300s.

First mechanical printing press developed by Gutenberg in Germany in AD 1450.

Christopher Columbus sets sail for the West Indies and discovers America in AD1492.

Glossary

Acropolis Fortified city that was built on a hill or high ground.

Agora Market and meeting place in center of Greek city.

Amphora Large, 2-handled pot.

Andron Dining room in a private house, used by men only.

Attic Dialect spoken by people in and around Athens.

Democracy System of government in which all citizens could have a say.

Diadochi Alexander's generals.

Gynaeceum Women's rooms in a private house.

Labrys Double-headed ax.

Libation An offering of wine.

Metic Foreigner in a city state.

Minoan Civilization which flourished on Crete.

Minotaur A monster who was half-man, half-bull.

Mycenaean Name given to people who dominated Greece from about 1600–1200 BC.

Oracle A shrine.

Phalanx Battle formation.

Trireme A Greek warship.

Tyrant A ruler with absolute power.

Index

Photographic credits:

All the pictures in this book are from C.M. Dixon Photo Resources apart from pages: front cover top, 15 top: Spectrum Colour Library; front cover bottom, 3 middle, 13: Roger Vlitos; 16 top: Robert Harding Picture Library; 19 right, 22 bottom left: Frank Spooner Pictures.